Steve and Susan,
Congratulations on your Florida purchase! Have a Blessed Christmas!

Candy
2015

ADVENT
FOR
INQUIRING MINDS

Interesting Facts

and

Inspiring Thoughts

about

Salvation History

Candy Kush

INTRODUCTION

The Jesse Tree is a traditional Advent custom of setting up a tree in the home and each day during Advent adding a symbolic ornament depicting an event in salvation history. In Isaiah 11:1 God promised that "a shoot shall sprout from the stump of Jesse, and from his roots a bud shall blossom." Jesse was the father of King David, and it is from this line of royalty that the Messiah was to come. The first chapter of Matthew lists the genealogy of Jesus and shows that his foster-father, Joseph, truly did come from the family tree of Jesse.

Because Jesus was a Jew, salvation history is really a history of the Jewish or Hebrew people. Today we are able to look at this history and see the many foreshadowings of Jesus, our Messiah. The Jewish people also recognize these prophecies, but they are still looking for their Messiah.

This book contains a topic or person for each day of Advent, beginning with creation and ending with the birth of Jesus. Each chapter has a Bible passage, an explanation and a prayer. They are suitable for family devotions or personal reflection.

There are also suggestions for ornaments. These can be collected items or created as a family project. They could be drawn, painted onto wooden rounds, scanned from the computer or formed from clay. There are some that can be printed from domestic-church.com. This time of year it is not too hard to find small, hanging, nativity scene ornaments that work well. Any kind of tree or base to hang things on will do. It is not necessary to have an actual tree and ornaments to use this book.

Because the number of days in Advent varies year by year, there are enough topics in this book to cover the longest Advent, but most years you will not use them all. Or you may find you will miss a day here or there. That's okay; each chapter can stand alone. The prophets are the best to skip, but feel free to pick the ones you like best. Sometimes during the holidays time really runs away with us. The final topics in the book are suitable for the days of the Christmas Season, from Christmas Day through the Baptism of Jesus. You may even want to save chapters like #28 Star for Epiphany and #26 Mary for January 1, the Solemnity of Mary.

Have a Happy Advent and a Blessed Christmas!

CONTENTS

1   Creation
2   Adam & Eve
3   Noah
4   Abraham
5   Melchizedek
6   Isaac
7   Jacob
8   Joseph
9   Moses
#10 Aaron
#11 Tabernacle
#12 Joshua
#13 Samuel
#14 Jesse
#15 David
#16 Solomon
#17 Elijah
#18 Jonah
#19 Isaiah
#20 Hezekiah
#21 Jeremiah
#22 Daniel
#23 Malachi
#24 Gabriel
#25 John
#26 Mary
#27 Joseph
#28 Star
#29 Jesus

#1 CREATION (small globe, sun, moon, stars)

Genesis 1:1-27

Happy New Year! The first Sunday of Advent marks the first day of a new liturgical year.

The Jewish people have always thought that God created the world in the fall, so they celebrate the beginning of the new year at Rosh Hashanah, which falls during our month of September or October. Because Genesis 1:5 says "evening came and morning followed", Jews also believe that each day begins at sunset; so they begin celebrating the night before the actual date of the holiday. Rosh Hashanah begins with the blowing of a ram's horn which they call a *shofar* and it is blown 100 times during the Rosh Hashanah service. In the Bible this is called the Feast of Trumpets.

The shofar represents the trumpet blast at the coronation of a king, and the Jews declare God to be King of the Universe on Rosh Hashanah. They teach that the continued existence of the universe depends upon God's "divine desire". It is His will which keeps the world functioning as we know it. If He withdrew His will from any creature or created thing, at that instant it would cease to exist.

Only God can truly create, that is, make something out of nothing. He doesn't use tools and supplies like an artist or designer, He simply wills it to be so and so it is.

It really doesn't matter if God made the world in six 24-hour days or six billion years, as long as we recognize Him as the ultimate Creator and Sustainer of it all. We owe praise to God not only for the beautiful world He gave us, but also for our very existence from day to day.

All numbers in the Bible have significance. The Jews loved to put numerical value on everything. Seven is God's favorite number. He made seven days in a week and made the seventh day the most special. We have seven sacraments. We will see more of this number as we travel through Advent.

PRAYER

God, our Father, You are truly great and we praise You for Your greatness. As we have just finished the Thanksgiving season, we thank You once more for Your great love for us, for the wonderful world You created, and for giving us life and sustaining us from day to day. As we begin the season of Advent, help us to recognize Your work in the world every day and to praise You for it.

Amen

#2 ADAM & EVE (apple, tree, snake)

Genesis 3:1-13

    Satan is a clever liar. There is always truth in what he tells us and tempts us to do. But he doesn't tell us about the consequences, the horrible result of our sins. When Satan told Eve her eyes would be opened and she would gain wisdom after eating the fruit, he was right. Her eyes were opened and she did gain wisdom, but it wasn't what she had expected. Up to this point, Eve and Adam knew no evil. Their lives were absolutely wonderful and perfect, what we all dream about: peace and tranquility and leisure.

    When Adam and Eve realized they were naked, it was a stunning revelation to them. Imagine being so self-unaware that you are not even conscious of your own body, let alone your desires. Their only thought was for the other person. After their sin, they became self-aware and self-ish. They passed that original sin on to us, and we find ourselves selfish and always looking out for number one. We are easily offended and get our feelings hurt and are disappointed when things don't go our way. Who would have guessed in the Garden of Eden that being self-aware could bring so much pain and discomfort?

    Well, God did. God knows everything and following His rules are always the best choice, even when it doesn't make sense to us and when following our own way seems like the smart way.

Once Adam and Eve allowed sin into their hearts, it was like they were kidnapped by Satan and God had to pay a ransom to get them back as His own children. God had to make a way for mankind to once again be sinless and pure. Thus, the plan of salvation began.

PRAYER

Lord Jesus, we ask for Your help during this Advent season and ask to always be enlightened by Your Grace and recognize Satan and his tactics for what they are. Help us not to succumb to his clever temptations and always to follow You and Your ways and the commandments set forth by Your Father. May Your angels guard and protect us from the evil one and his many followers. Fill us with Your love and grace and empty us of our selfishness, especially during this season when we look forward to Your coming at Christmas.

      Amen

#3 NOAH (ark, rainbow)

Genesis 6:11-14; 7:6-12, 17-23

Yesterday we saw evil enter the world and today we see that it has totally run amuck and taken over nearly all of mankind. All humans on earth except for Noah and his family have been duped by Satan's half-truths. So much so, that God must destroy them all.

Most major civilizations have some version of the Noah story in their folklore, which helps us to believe it is a genuinely true story passed on through the generations and not just a folktale. It is also a reasonable way to explain the end of the dinosaur age. Until the time of the flood, there had never been rain on the earth – it was watered by dew and springs and was probably a very humid climate, like what we see in dinosaur movies. A haze likely covered the earth, which protected it from harmful rays of the sun and made living things grow very large. Right before the Noah story, Genesis 6:1-4 tells us of giants living on the earth.

The story of Noah gives many figurative glimpses into the future of the salvation of mankind. First, there are the forty days of rain. Biblical periods of trial seem to center around the number 40. The Israelites spent 40 years wandering in the desert before they could enter the Promised Land. Jesus spent 40 days in the wilderness fasting and preparing for His ministry. And we have 40 days of Lent before Easter.

Next, there is Noah being saved by his passage through the water. We are washed clean of original sin and saved by passing through the waters of baptism.

And then there is the ark. It safely carried Noah to a kind of rebirth on the earth. The Israelites had the Ark of the Covenant which they carried with them into the Promised Land, ushering in a new age for them. Mary was a kind of ark, carrying Jesus to His birth on the earth which began a new age for all of mankind.

So what happened to Noah's ark? Many believe it is buried under the ice on Mount Ararat (Genesis 8:4) in modern day Turkey near the border of Armenia. There have been many expeditions there, but none that have found anything conclusive. Many things of God remain hidden. Jesus hides Himself in the bread and wine. His birth was hidden in a lowly stable. Perhaps He just wants us to search for Him like the magi did.

PRAYER

Dear Father, we acknowledge You as Judge of all the earth and hope that we may be found holy in your sight as was Noah. Help us always to follow Your leadings and instructions as Noah did, so that we may be saved. We know that You have given us a free will to choose evil or good. Help us to always choose good, to choose what pleases You, to live our lives in a holy manner, so that we may spend eternity with You. Help us to remain steadfast to our call no matter the cost. And we ask for the intercession of Noah on our behalf.

Amen

#4 ABRAHAM   (camel, tent, palm tree)

Genesis 12:1-8

    Abraham was an Arab sheik very much like those we see in the movies. He lived in lavish tents with lots of servants to wait on him and take care of his large herds of animals as he traveled around the desert. He left the city of Ur (located in present day Iraq) with his father, Terah, as part of the disbursement after the Tower of Babel incident (Genesis 11:1-9). They traveled as far as Haran and after Terah died, Abraham moved on to the land of Canaan, now called Israel.

    God spoke directly to Abraham and made a covenant, a special agreement, with him. God promised that if Abraham would take God for his own, God would bless him and give him many descendents and all the land of Canaan in which they could live. We know the end of the story, that God kept His end of the deal and blessed Abraham with not just one, but two families of descendents; thus we call him Father Abraham. Through his son, Isaac, the Jewish people came to be; and through his son, Ishmael, the Arab people came to be. Isaac and Ishmael fought as young boys and the Jews and Arabs still fight today.

    Back in those ancient times, the father of the family was also the priest who offered sacrifices for the family. When Noah came out of the ark after the flood, he offered an animal sacrifice to God. After Abraham made his covenant with God, he offered a sacrifice. Sacrifice literally means a gift, and in ancient times all cultures offered sacrifices to their gods. It seems people have always had the urge to give gifts to God.

Jesus descended from Abraham and was both the priest and the victim of the ultimate sacrifice. We remember that sacrifice and the covenant it sealed whenever we celebrate the mass. God still promises that if we will take Him for our God, He will bless us, forgive us of all wrongdoing and take us to heaven to be with Him forever.

PRAYER

Dear Lord Jesus, we thank You for the great sacrifice You made on the cross, offering Yourself as the perfect gift to Your Father. We thank You that You always keep Your promises and we ask that we will remain faithful to You so that we will be worthy of Your promises and spend eternity with You in heaven. May we follow the example of Abraham's righteousness and trust in You, and we ask for his intercession on our behalf.

Amen

#5 MELCHIZEDEK (chalice, wine, bread, wheat)

Genesis 14:13-20

Today we see Abraham acting like the tribal chieftain that he is. His nephew, Lot, was kidnapped by four kings and Abraham takes a fighting force of 318 men from among his household servants and recovers Lot as well as other captives and possessions from the evil kings.

On his way home, Abraham stops to pay tribute to the King of Salem, Melchizedek. Most of us are familiar with the Jewish greeting, *shalom*, which means peace. *Salem* and *shalom* are the same basic Hebrew word, so Melchizedek was the King of Peace. (The Prophet Isaiah calls the Messiah the Prince of Peace in Isaiah 9:5.) Today we know the city of Salem as Jeru-salem, city of peace.

So who was Melchizedek? No one knows for sure. Some speculate that he was Shem, one of Noah's sons. If we add up all the years in the Genesis genealogies, we find that Shem was still alive at the time of Abraham. Hebrews 7:3 tells us that Melchizedek had no beginning or end and that Jesus is a priest of the same order.

Melchizedek makes an offering of bread and wine. That sounds familiar, doesn't it? At the Last Supper, Jesus offered bread and wine. When we celebrate the mass, we have bread and wine.

Abraham gives an offering to Melchizedek of one-tenth of all the booty he seized in the battle. Still today we consider a tithe of one-tenth of our income as belonging to God, to be used for the needs of the church and its priests.

This is an important precept we should not neglect. One can never outgive God. He promises to pay us back with even more blessings. *Give and gifts will be given to you; a good measure, packed together, shaken down, and overflowing, will be poured into your lap. For the measure with which you measure will in return be measured out to you.* (Luke 6:38)

PRAYER

Jesus, our Lord and Savior, we acknowledge You as our Priest and King, the only true King of Peace. We thank You for the offering of Yourself, which we celebrate at every mass. Help us to never take Your offering for granted. Help us never forget the offering we owe to You and to do our part to please You. Help us to always give You the honor due to You as our King.

Amen

#6 ISAAC (ram, bundle of sticks)

Genesis 22:1-13

    Isaac was the son God promised to Abraham, but he wasn't born until Abraham was 99 years old. After waiting for this child of promise for so long, it seems very strange that God would tell Abraham to kill him.

    We have learned that a sacrifice is a gift (#4 Abraham), but it is actually more than that. In a true sacrifice to God, the gift is destroyed so that it is no longer able to be used by humans; it is a way of giving it back to God. So in Old Testament times, an animal sacrifice was killed and burned, bread and grain sacrifices were burned and a wine sacrifice was poured out on the ground. The original Latin word *vicima,* the root for our word *victim,* meant the gift that was offered.

    So when God asked for Isaac, He was asking for a gift, Abraham's most cherished possession. God wanted to know if Abraham loved Him more than anything. God still asks the same of us. Do we love God more than anything, even our most cherished possession or family member or friend?

    Isaac prefigures Jesus Christ more than anyone we have learned about so far. They were both the very beloved sons of their fathers. They were both offered as sacrifices, though Isaac was spared at the last minute. They both carried the wood on which they were laid and they both carried that wood up a hill to the place of the sacrifice. And they both did all of this willingly, trusting in their fathers.

    There is another interesting circumstance in this story. The mountain Isaac and Abraham climbed to make their sacrifice, Mount Moriah, is the very same mountain on which the temple was later built by King Solomon, where thousands of sacrifices were offered every year.

And one more note: the Jews believe that the sacrifice of Isaac happened on Rosh Hashanah, the Jewish New Year (#1 Creation). It is another reason they blow the shofar, a ram's horn, because a ram took Isaac's place.

PRAYER

Our Lord and Savior, we see that there are no coincidences with You. All things are planned by You for our ultimate good. We want to trust and love you the way Abraham did and the way Isaac trusted his father. We know that You will ask nothing of us that we are not capable of doing and that if we will only trust You, You will work all things for our good. Help us to love and trust you more and more with each passing day during this Advent season.

Amen

#7 JACOB (angel, angel wings)

Genesis 32:23-32

Jacob was the son of Isaac and the grandson of Abraham. It is likely that as a child, Jacob hung around Abraham and heard stories of God. The Bible tells us Jacob stayed home while his twin brother, Esau, went out to hunt. Abraham lived to be 175 and was 99 when Isaac was born and Isaac was 60 when Jacob was born. That means Abraham was around for the first 16 years of Jacob's life.

Esau was the first of the twins to be born, and you may recall the story of Jacob deceiving his father in order to receive the blessing that was customarily given in those days to the eldest son (Genesis 27). Esau should have received it, but instead Jacob did. Along with the blessing, the son received a double portion of the inheritance. As we might expect, Esau was very angry when he found out and wanted to kill Jacob, so Jacob ran far away to his uncle's home. While there, he married two wives and ended up with 12 sons and one daughter.

In today's reading, Jacob and his family are on their way back to his childhood home. He meets an angel as he crosses the Jordan River into Canaan. It has been speculated that this angel was the same one God put at the entrance of the Garden of Eden when He sent Adam and Eve away. In Jewish folklore, the angel Jacob fights with is named Samael, Esau's guardian angel, and the reason the angel hurts his hip is because Jacob fights so well, the angel can't believe he is human. So the angel looks for a hip joint – angels have no joints.

Jacob wrestles with this angel and begs for a blessing. He seems to be willing to do anything for a blessing. He lied to his father for one and now he fights with an angel for one.

The angel does bless him and changes his name from Jacob to Israel. *El* are the first letters in the Hebrew name for God, *Elohim.* So whenever we see *el* in a Hebrew name, it means *God.* The *isra* part means *you contended,* so *Israel* means *you fought with God.*

The nation of Israel takes its name from Jacob, and his 12 sons become the 12 tribes of Israel.

PRAYER

Our God, Elohim, we thank You for the rich heritage You gave us in the Patriarchs of the Old Testament. We, too, beg for Your blessing upon us today and throughout this new liturgical year that begins with Advent. Prosper us as You did Jacob. Prosper our work and prosper our spirits so that our love for You will increase, and we will give all of the praise and glory to You.

Amen

#8 JOSEPH (pyramid, Pharaoh, dream catcher, multi-colored coat)
Genesis 45:1-8

Of Jacob's 12 sons, Joseph was the favorite. This was because Joseph was the son of his favorite wife, Rachel, who died giving birth to Joseph's only full-blooded brother, Benjamin. All of Joseph's half-brothers were so jealous that they decided to get rid of him and sold him to slave traders. Most of us know the story of how Joseph moved from being a slave to being the most powerful ruler in Egypt next to the Pharaoh himself. His position enabled him to save his entire family from starving to death during a seven-year famine (Genesis 37-45).

Joseph is a strong foreshadowing of Jesus Christ. Firstly, there is his name. We remember that Jesus' foster-father was also named Joseph, a name which means *increase.*

The Genesis Joseph was betrayed and sold for 20 pieces of silver, the price of a slave. Jesus was also sold for the price of a slave at 30 pieces of silver. That is a 50% inflation rate over a period of 2000 years!

Both Joseph and Jesus were taken to Egypt by someone else. They were both convicted criminals. They both saved an entire world from death. Joseph saved the then-known world from starvation and physical death, and Jesus saved all mankind from spiritual death. In fact, the name *Jesus* is a Greek form of the name *Joshua* which means *savior.*

Joseph had everything his family needed to survive. But they had to go to him to get it. In the same way, Jesus has done everything necessary for our salvation, but we need to go to Him to get it. We need to ask for it just like Joseph's brothers had to ask. And like they asked Joseph for forgiveness, we need to ask for forgiveness from Jesus.

PRAYER

Lord Jesus, we recognize You as the Savior of the world. We humbly come before You and beg for Your forgiveness of all of the times we have offended You. Please grant us Your gift of salvation so that we might spend eternity with You in heaven. Help us to always recognize Your Providence in every situation and know that even when things look bleak, as they did for Joseph, You are in control and will work out all things for our good.
        Amen

#9 MOSES (law tablet, basket, pyramid, pharaoh)

Exodus 19:16-20

We all know and love the story of Baby Moses in the bulrushes, saved by the princess (Exodus 2). By command of the Pharaoh, all Jewish baby boys born at that time were drowned in the Nile River. Jesus, too, was saved as a baby. King Herod ordered all infant boys under two years of age to be killed, but Mary and Joseph escaped with Jesus to, of all places, Egypt, the home of Moses.

Moses became a great leader and led the Israelites out of their slavery in Egypt to the Promised Land of Canaan, modern day Israel. But before he could do that, he spent 40 years in the desert, living the solitary life of a shepherd. There, God prepared him to be a leader and he learned how to survive in the wilderness; a good thing since he spent another 40 years in charge of 600,000 Israelites wandering about in the wilderness. Jesus spent 40 days in the desert wilderness preparing to lead His kingdom. We have already noted that the number 40 is symbolic as a time of testing and trial (#3 Noah).

God gave the law to Moses because God loved the people and wanted them to be happy and live in peace. If you buy a new piece of electronics or an appliance, it works best if you follow the instructions that come with it. Our lives are best if we follow the instructions God gave us. Think how safe and peaceful and happy our world would be if every person followed God's laws.

Jesus said in Matthew 5:17 that He came to fulfill the law. One way He did this was to clarify it for us. He said our first duty was to God and then to our neighbor. He gave us the story of the Good Samaritan to demonstrate. Jesus also established His Church to interpret and apply His law. The laws of the Church help us follow God's law more perfectly on a day-to-day basis. They give us the minimum requirement for holiness. But we should have no limits to our own growth in holiness.

PRAYER

Lord God, our Father, we thank You for the gift of Your law and the guidance that it gives us. We thank You for the gift of Your son and the love that He gives to us and to His Church. We thank You for the Church and the foundation it gives us. Help us to follow these guides so that our lives will be holy and pleasing to You.

Amen

#10 AARON (almonds)

Numbers 17:16-26: 18:1

    We have seen that in the Genesis days, the father of the family acted as the priest and made sacrifices to God for his entire family. (#4 Abraham) During their time in Egypt, the Israelites were not allowed to sacrifice animals. But once they left Egypt and were wandering in the wilderness, they again could offer animal sacrifices. It would have been utterly chaotic if every family was killing and burning animals willy-nilly, so God established a High Priest and helper priests to do this on behalf of all the people. The man God chose to be High Priest was Aaron, Moses' brother. Aaron's sons would be the priests and their sons would be priests and so on. From here on, all Jewish priests had to come from this family; the family, or tribe, of Levi. Levi was one of the 12 sons of Jacob, a many-times-over-great-grandfather of Moses and Aaron.
    We have learned that a sacrifice is a gift and that it needs to be destroyed so that no human can use it; it belongs completely to God (#6 Isaac). The person who offers the sacrifice is the priest, and he must have the authority to do this. The Genesis men had the authority because they were the heads of their families. Aaron and his sons had this authority because they were appointed by God, as we see in today's scripture reading. Our priests today have this authority because they have been ordained by their bishops to offer the sacrifice of the mass. Protestant ministers are not called priests because they do not offer the sacrifice of the mass.

Jesus is the real High Priest. Remember Melchizedek? (#5 Melchizedek) The Bible tells us Jesus is a priest of his order, getting His authority directly from God, His Father. He offered the sacrifice of Himself. Before Aaron could offer sacrifices, he had to do cleansing rituals and follow specific rules so that he could stand before God without sin to offer the sacrifices. Jesus was totally without sin, making Him the perfect High Priest. His sinlessness also made him the perfect Victim and the perfect King.

PRAYER

Jesus, our High Priest, we thank You once again for the gift of Yourself on the cross. We thank You that You were worthy to offer the gift of Yourself and You were the perfect, sinless victim; and by that sacrifice You purchased our salvation from the fires of hell. May we never take Your willing sacrifice for granted and always live in a manner worthy of Your sacrifice and great love for us.

Amen

#11 TABERNACLE (tent)

Exodus 25:1-9; 40:34-35

Shortly after Moses received the stone tablets engraved with the Ten Commandments, God gave him directions on building a home to keep them in. But this home was not just for the stone tablets; it was to be a house for God Himself to dwell in.

Because the Israelites were wandering rather aimlessly about the desert wilderness, the house of God had to be transportable. So it was really more of a tent than a building. The main structure, the Sanctuary, had three walls made of wooden planks covered in gold, standing upright edge to edge. Over these were draped four layers of curtains, woven in blue, purple and scarlet, embroidered with angels. For a roof, there was a covering of woven goat-hair, then a layer of ram-skins and on top, a third layer of badger-skins to protect it from the weather.

The inside was divided into two rooms. The first was the Holy Place which contained three pieces of furniture: the altar of incense, the table of shew-bread and the golden lampstand which contained seven (God's favorite number again!) branches which held small bowls of olive oil. The priests went in here twice daily to offer incense and keep the oil lamps burning.

A veil or curtain divided the Holy Place from the inner-room, called the Holy of Holies. The only furniture in this room was the Ark of the Covenant, which held the Ten Commandments inside. As time went on, two more items were placed in the Ark: a piece of manna and Aaron's staff (#10 Aaron). It was in the Holy of Holies that the Glory of God, the *shekinah* dwelt.

The Ark was like a throne for God; its lid was called the Mercy Seat. Only the high priest was allowed to enter the Holy of Holies and only on one day of the year, the Day of Atonement, Yom Kippur. He would take the blood from a slaughtered bullock and goat and sprinkle it seven times (yes, seven!) in front of the Mercy Seat to ask God's forgiveness for the sins of all the people. It was customary for the high priest to attach bells to the bottom of his robe so the people could hear him working inside; and also to have a rope tied to his ankle so if he passed out or died in there, he could be pulled out. No one else was allowed in.

The whole Sanctuary was surrounded by a courtyard, and it was in this courtyard that the ritual washings and animal slaughtering and burning took place. It had only one entrance on the east side.

This was God's dwelling place until King Solomon built a permanent temple (#16 Solomon). Solomon's Temple had the same layout as that of the Tabernacle.

Matthew 27:51 says that at the moment Jesus died on the cross "the veil of the sanctuary was torn in two from top to bottom." Matthew means that we no longer need a high priest to go into God's presence for us. We all have access to God's Glory and Mercy Seat. Jesus, who was both the priest and the victim, opened the way for us. Not only can we approach God anytime, but we do not need to bring Him an animal sacrifice. The only sacrifice He wants is our willing heart.

PRAYER

Holy and Merciful God, we are so thankful for the gift of Your Son, the perfect sacrifice, who opened the way to Your Glory. Thank You for making us all priests in that we can go directly into Your Presence. Help us to be worthy to serve You and Your Son. May we be eager to enter Your Presence often.

Amen

#12 JOSHUA (sword)

Joshua 1:1-11

Joshua became the leader of the Israelites after Moses died. Moses and his generation were not allowed to enter the Promised Land of Canaan because they doubted God's promise and His ability to help them be victorious in battles against the Canaanites. But Joshua led them into the land and they conquered the pagans who lived there. We remember the story of the Israelites marching around the city of Jericho for seven days and then the walls fell down (Joshua 6). Joshua was more of an army general leading the troops than he was a political judge, as Moses had been.

God had promised this land to Abraham, along with the promise to make of his seed a great nation. At the time of Abraham's death, the only land he owned was a small burial plot he had purchased to bury his wife, Sarah. His "nation" consisted of one son, a daughter-in-law, and two grandsons. (Ishmael had left to make his own nation – that of the Arabs.) When Grandson Jacob traveled to Egypt, he had 72 in his household. But 400 and some years later, the Israelites number in the hundreds of thousands. They *are* a great nation, but they have no land on which to live. The story of Joshua is a fulfillment of the rest of God's promise to Abraham. It is also a prophecy of how Christianity, in a spiritual sense, gradually conquered the world like the Israelites, in a physical sense, gradually conquered the land.

In our time, it is difficult to understand the Israelites barging into someone else's country and taking it over, slaughtering all who live there. It reminds us of today's terrorists, who consider theirs a holy war. The

Israelites did fight a holy war in that God commanded them to do it, which seems contrary to the God of love we worship. But we must understand the Israelite conquest in the context of the ancient times in which they lived.

War was a yearly spring and summer activity in those days and every king led his people in battle. Each city-state had their own patron god in whose name the people fought and who was greatly honored after a victory. The conquered people were often killed as a sacrifice of thanksgiving to the god. Remember that in a true sacrifice, the victim must be destroyed so that it belongs only to the god and is unusable for humans (#6 Isaac).

The Israelites' God, our God, was different from the other gods of the time in that He actually led and fought in the battles. He was a Warrior God. He made the walls of Jericho fall, he confused enemy troops, he sent lightening and plagues upon the enemy. The people of Canaan were struck with fear at the news of the approaching army of Israelites. Everyone was aware that the Israelite God was more powerful than any of the Canaanite gods. Of course, we know that their gods were not gods at all, just idols of stone or wood, and our God is the only true God.

So, the lesson for us is that our God is still a Warrior God. He will still fight your battles for you. IF you trust Him. Today's Bible passage from Joshua is full of wonderful promises, just as good for us as they were for Joshua and his people. If we observe God's law, we will succeed wherever we go (vs. 7). God will never leave us or forsake us (vs. 5). Do not fear or be dismayed for God is with you (vs. 9).

PRAYER

Holy God, we praise Your name. We are in awe of the many wonderful things You have done for Your people and those that have loved You throughout the ages. We thank You for Your wonderful promises; may we always keep them in our hearts. We acknowledge You as our Warrior God, and ask You to fight our battles for us today and every day. Be with us as we face the temptations to selfishness and to respond to others in an unkind way. Smooth the way before us in our troubled relationships. And help us to always follow Your will in all that we do and then trust You as the Supreme God over all circumstances.

Amen

#13 SAMUEL (Samuel figure, Ark of the Covenant)
1 Samuel 3:1-10, 19-21

Typical of the time period, Samuel's father had two wives. One wife had many children, but Samuel's mother, Hannah, had none. Similarly to the stories of Abraham, Jacob, and their wives, once again the childless wife was the favorite wife. Hannah begged God to give her a son and promised to give him back to God if He answered her prayer. God did answer her prayer, making Samuel another child of promise. Once he was old enough, Hannah took Samuel to the temple, a very elaborate tent made of animal skins; the actual temple building had not yet been built (#11 Tabernacle). Hannah left Samuel there to live with the High Priest, Eli.

Amazingly enough, Samuel slept in the sanctuary near the Ark of the Covenant, a very holy place. The Ark was kind of like God's throne; God's glory, called *shekinah* in Hebrew, would sit on top of the Ark in a cloud of smoke. It doesn't seem like a person could spend so much time in the presence of God and not be called to action.

During the years between Joshua and Samuel, Israel had no real leader except God Himself. People lived in their city-states and the country was not really united, except in that people would travel to the temple for holy days to make sacrifices. When some neighboring country would cause trouble during their yearly spring/summer warpath, God would raise up a judge to lead an army against them. Samson, Gideon and Deborah were some of the judges during this time.

When God called Samuel to be His prophet, things began to change. Samuel traveled throughout the land, preaching and making sacrifices, and people everywhere knew and respected him as the Voice of God. We can be sure that when God called Samuel as a boy, Samuel had no idea what God had in mind and no idea that God would make him into such a great prophet. But it was Samuel's willingness that allowed it to be so.

Samuel prefigures Christ in that he also was a child of promise, born rather miraculously; he was willing to be used by God and he spoke God's words. Samuel's sleeping in the temple reminds us of a line in the Bible used to describe the Messiah: *Zeal for your house consumes me* (John 2:17 & Psalm 69:10).

We should all be zealous for God and eager to go to His house, eager to worship Him and learn from Him. We should also be willing to do whatever He calls us to do. We should daily ask Him, "What do you want me to do?" We should ask this in the long-term sense as in seeking a vocation and in the short-term sense as in "Who can I help today?" When we sense His desire for us, we should say, "Here I am, Lord."

PRAYER
God, our Heavenly Father, we thank You again for the rich heritage of our faith, for the examples of the patriarchs and prophets, especially for Samuel, who shows us how to be willing to follow You. Help us to listen to Your voice and always to answer Your call with a "Yes, here I am, Lord."
Amen

#14 JESSE (branch)

1 Samuel 16:4-13

Today we finally have the guy after whom our Advent tree is named, Jesse. Jesse was from the tribe of Judah and lived in Bethlehem. He was a shepherd with herds of sheep and goats and he had eight sons. His genealogy is given twice in the Old Testament (Ruth 4:18-22; 1 Chronicles 2:5-12), and again in the genealogy of Jesus in Matthew 1:1-17. He has a dubious background in that women of questionable reputation are included in his genealogy. Very rarely are women mentioned in a Biblical genealogy, but the genealogy of Jesus includes five of them.

Jesse's grandmother was Ruth, the famous Moabite woman who moved to Israel with her mother-in-law and married Boaz (Ruth 1-4). Jesse's great-grandmother is also well known, Rahab. She was the harlot who hid the Israelite spies when they came into Jericho to scout the city before the battle. She and her family were saved before the walls fell down (Joshua 2 & 6). And Jesse's grandmother six generations before Rahab had children with her father-in-law, Judah, Jesse's seven-times-great-grandfather and one of the original 12 sons of Jacob. None of these women were Jewish. It's all a little scandalous, but as we keep seeing, God takes bad and makes it good.

Jesse does not seem to be one of the leaders of Bethlehem who comes out to meet Samuel, but he is invited to the sacrificial meal along with the city leaders. It is likely that he was just a rather poor guy, and David, who ends up being the Chosen One, is the least significant of the family, not even allowed to come to dinner. As the youngest son, it is left to him to stay in the pastures and watch the flocks. It is possible that the phrase *son of Jesse* could have had a derogatory connotation. But once again God turned things topsy-turvy and that phrase became a matter of pride when David became the greatest king in all of Israel's history.

Through his foster-father, Joseph, Jesus is a *son of Jesse* because Joseph descended through the Judah/Jesse family line. When we speak of the *Tree of Jesse*, we mean his family tree, all of his ancestors and descendents. The sons and grandsons of David were the kings of Israel for many years, but eventually the people turned to idolatry. So God punished them by allowing foreigners to conquer the land; the *sons of Jesse* were no longer kings. That is the *stump of Jesse*, and Jesus is the *shoot* and the *bud that blossomed* from the *stump* to which Isaiah referred in his prophecy: *A shoot shall sprout from the stump of Jesse, and from his roots a bud shall blossom.* (Isaiah 11:1)

PRAYER

Jesus, our Great King, we thank You that through Your humble beginning and ancestry, You have made it clear to us that Your Kingdom is accessible to all, whether rich or poor or respected or despised. We thank You for Your great love for us which you showed when you came to earth into meager circumstances and gave us the gift of Yourself. We thank You that You can turn any ugly situation into a way for You to be glorified. Help us not to take any of these gifts for granted and to always trust in Your Divine Providence.

Amen

#15 DAVID (crown, king)

2 Samuel 5:1-5

Even people who know very little about the Bible usually know the story of David and Goliath. When David, son of Jesse, was still a teenager, he was anointed king, killed a lion and a bear with his hands and killed a giant Philistine with a small stone (1 Samuel 17). As he grew into manhood, he became a valiant warrior, vanquishing thousands and thousands of enemy troops. As king he led the army into battle every spring, constantly defeating the neighboring pagan tribes and enlarging the territory of Israel. Eventually, all of their enemies were defeated and peace and prosperity reigned throughout the land. Sounds like a fairy tale, doesn't it? No wonder David was Israel's favorite and best king. He makes a perfect foreshadowing of the promised Messiah.

But David's heroics in battle were not what made God favor him. In yesterday's scripture reading we read that God does not look at the outward appearance, He looks at the heart. 1 Samuel 13:14 tells us that David was a man after God's own heart. Lest we put David on too high a pedestal, we need to look into his later years when he did things he should not have done. He sinned with Bathsheba and then had her husband killed. His children ran amuck: one molested his half-sister, another killed his half-brother, one tried to defile David's harem and usurp the throne. But David had a heart tuned to God and when he realized his sin, he repented with true sorrow for what he had done.

God loved David and rewarded him with the promise that his royal throne would last forever through his descendents (2 Samuel 7:12-16). This promise found its fulfillment in Jesus, the Messiah. But David was also punished for his sins; God told him the sword would never depart from his house (2 Samuel 12:10). This was fulfilled in grandsons whose years as ruler were marred by wars and fighting. Never again did Israel enjoy the peace they had while David was king. Even to this day, Israel is troubled with terrorist attacks, battles, and skirmishes with their neighbors.

That is why everyone looks forward to the endless reign of the Messiah. We all yearn for peace and prosperity, for unity and understanding among all people, especially those in our own lives. But we can work toward this goal; we know the song, *Let there be peace on earth, and let it begin with me.*

PRAYER

Our King and Messiah, we worship You today as King and Lord of all, the promised Messiah who came to us in a lowly stable rather than a magnificent palace. Help us to be people after Your own heart as David was. Help us to love You and be truly sorry for our sins and to be quick to repent when we offend Your goodness. Make us people of peace, able to pass that peace on to those we meet.

                    Amen

#16 SOLOMON (temple, king)

1 Kings 5:9-19

    The tenth and last son of King David was Solomon. His mother was the scandalous Bathsheba, who, once again, seems to be the favorite wife. It was very unusual for the youngest son to succeed his father as king; it was usually the first-born son. But David had promised Bathsheba that her son would become king. Her first son died at birth, so her next son, Solomon, became king.

    Until the reign of Solomon, God was still worshiped in the tent-like tabernacle. King David greatly desired to build a permanent temple building, but it was Solomon who finally built it on the site David had picked. Amazingly enough, it was built on the same mountain on which Abraham had offered Isaac (#6 Isaac.) It took seven and a half years to build, and when it was done, Solomon built himself a palace.

    King Solomon is well known for his great wisdom. When he became king, God told him He would give Solomon anything he wanted. Solomon chose wisdom so that he could rule well. God was pleased with his choice and gave him incredible wisdom along with wealth, power and peace. During his reign, the then-known world respected Israel as a world power in a way they never had before nor did they again during the reigns of any of his descendents. Israel had a huge army, ambitious building programs, and Solomon lived in kingly opulence and luxury. In this way, Solomon is a type of the Messiah; a great king who rules with wisdom, justice, wealth, power and firm control.

But Solomon was not the Messiah, and he went the way of many powerful men. In order to support his great army, building programs and luxurious lifestyle, he over-taxed his subjects, making them poorer while he grew richer. All of the healthy young men were drafted into service in the army. Revolts among the people were quelled ruthlessly. He began a system of forced labor gangs to build the temple and his palace. He had a weakness for women and we are told he had 1000 wives and loved them all. He made peaceful, political alliances by marrying princesses from nearby countries, and then allowed them to worship their false gods. His own heart was turned toward these idols, whether to please his wives or for political gain, we do not know. Perhaps in his great wisdom he saw truths within these other religions which he wanted to follow, but then became sucked in to what was not true. Even though we are not kings with great power, we need to guard our hearts against tolerance that allows us to accept what is false along with the truth.

The Jewish people have always put great significance on numbers. The number of God is seven. The number of incompleteness, or evil, is six, one number less than God's number. You may recall the *Mark of the Beast* from Revelation 13:18. The Beast's number is 666. The Bible tells us that the number of steps on Solomon's throne was 6 (1 Kings 10:10), and he received a yearly tribute of 666 talents of gold (1Kings 10:14). Solomon began his reign as a wise man who found favor in God's eyes, but he ended it as a greedy, selfish, idol worshipping dictator. There is even some historical evidence that suggests he dabbled in the black magical arts.

God could not allow all of this to go unpunished, so he rose up adversaries in nearby countries who were old enemies of King David. A man named Jeroboam, who worked for Solomon, led a rebellion against him, and later became king of the northern half of the country, called Israel; while Solomon's son ruled only the small southern part, called Judah. The kingdom was divided because of Solomon's sin, and it stayed divided for many, many years. God is merciful, and it is possible that the kingdom could have been spared had Solomon or even his son truly repented. But they did not, and God's punishment stood. There are many great lessons here for us: guard against the sins of greed, lust, selfishness, thirst for power, and trusting in our own wisdom; do not trust the half-truths of Satan and our own minds; be quick to repent when we have done wrong, be sure that God's righteous judgment demands a penalty for sin.

PRAYER
Holy and righteous God, we praise You for the wisdom You gave to Solomon and that it is available to us for the asking. It is one of the gifts of Your Spirit. We ask for that gift now. Fill our minds with Your Wisdom so that Your will may become our own. Infuse our hearts with Your love; love for You and love for our neighbor, so that we will not live our lives in selfishness, but will impart Your love to all we meet.
Amen

#17 ELIJAH   (mantle, raven, urn, fire)

2 Kings 2:8-14

We have now reached the Age of the Prophets, and Elijah was the most popular and colorful of them all. It was Elijah who met with Jesus and Moses at the Transfiguration (Luke 9:29-36). Still today the Jews set an empty place for Elijah at their Passover or Seder meals. He represents the Messiah for whom they still wait. They expect Elijah to reappear to announce the Kingdom of the Messiah. For Christians, John the Baptist was the *Elijah* who proclaimed that Jesus was that Messiah.

Several generations after Solomon, the country was still divided, and King Ahab ruled in Israel, the northern kingdom, with his wife, Jezebel. We have all heard of *her.* Jezebel turned the heart of her husband and much of the country towards the worship of the idol, Baal. Elijah angered them by condemning their false worship. They, especially Jezebel, wanted to kill Elijah, so he fled into the wilderness where he lived by a brook and was fed by ravens that brought him food. This sounds a lot like John the Baptist who lived in the wilderness and ate honey and locusts. John also angered a king and his wife, Herod and Herodias, who *did* have him killed (Mark 6:17-29).

When the brook dried up, Elijah lived with a poor widow and her son, and they were miraculously fed for a year with one small pot of flour and an urn of oil. The son died, but Elijah raised him back to life.

Elijah came out of hiding to carry on a strange battle; he alone against 850 prophets of Baal. They built two stone altars and slaughtered two animals and then prayed to their gods for fire to consume the sacrifice. Baal didn't show up. Elijah teased the prophets and said maybe their god was asleep or on a journey or going to the bathroom. But Elijah's God, our God, did show up. Elijah dumped 12 jars of water on the altar, just to make it more difficult to catch fire. God sent down fire . . . lots of it . . . which consumed not only the animal and the wood, but also the water and the stones!

Elijah did not die a natural death. A chariot of fire came out of heaven, picked him up and carried him off into the clouds. His side-kick, Elisha, watched him go, caught the mantle Elijah dropped down to him, and became his successor and another great prophet.

Elijah is a great hero for us. He never gave up. He trusted God when his life was threatened, when he had no food and when he was hugely outnumbered. And every time, God took care of him, as He will do for us if we trust Him.

PRAYER

Our one and only true God, we praise You for the great God that You are, that You do not sleep or go on journeys, that You always hear us when we call upon You, that You are powerful enough to send immense fire to earth, but small enough to live within our hearts. Help us to recognize You wherever You are, and to recognize those who speak in Your name, and not to be deceived by false prophets or their false gods, those subtle things that can get in the way of our relationship with You. Make us grow in holiness so that we can be spiritual warriors like Elijah and win our battles against evil.

      Amen

#18 JONAH (fish)

Jonah 1:1-7, 13-15; 2:1

The story of Jonah and the whale is very popular and most of us have been familiar with it since we were very young. God told him to go to Nineveh to preach, but Jonah tried to avoid God by boarding a ship heading the opposite direction. God sent a huge fish to swallow Jonah as a punishment for Jonah's disobedience. We do not know what kind of fish, maybe a whale, maybe a shark, maybe a prehistoric-type of sea monster. He remained inside for three days and nights. It is amazing he wasn't digested. The smell must have been really, really bad! Jonah's undigested body must have given the fish a bellyache because it vomited him up onto dry land and Jonah wisely decided to do what God wanted and went to Nineveh.

Jonah is mentioned as a prophet of God in 2 Kings 14:25, which puts him living around the year 820 B.C. Nineveh was the capitol of Assyria. The Assyrians were especially fearsome (more on them in #19 Isaiah), so we can understand why Jonah did not want to go there. This story probably happened about a hundred years before the Assyrians conquered the northern kingdom of Israel.

Jesus Himself mentioned Jonah in His teaching. He said that He would remain in the bowels of the earth for three days just as Jonah was in the belly of the fish for three days (Matthew 12:40). We have noted before that numbers are very significant in scripture, and the number 3 is especially important. It is the number of completeness; as in beginning, middle, end; or past, present, future. It is the number of God– there are three persons in the Trinity. It is also symbolic of resurrection. Interestingly, Genesis 1 tells us the dry land emerged from the waters on the third day of creation and Jonah emerged from the water also on the third day. Jesus raised three people from the dead: Jairus' daughter, the son of the widow in Nain, and Lazarus. Jesus' ministry lasted three years, He died at 3:00 and He came to life on the third day. Peter denied Christ three times and then affirmed his love three times. Jonah 3:3 tells us it took three days to walk through Nineveh. The number 3 is used more times in scripture than any other number except 7 (God's *favorite* number).

    Jesus also said that Jonah was a sign for the people and that at the final judgment, the men of Nineveh would speak against the Jews of Jesus' time (Matthew 12:39,41; Luke 11:29-30). The *sign* of which Jesus speaks is that Jonah was called to preach to Gentiles, non-Jews, and they repented and were saved. The Jews were very narrow minded, thinking that God was only for them. But the story of Jonah shows that God is for all people who will give their hearts to Him. The Jews in New Testament times refused to believe in Jesus, so the Gospel was opened up to the Gentiles who did believe, as was foreshadowed by Jonah and the Ninevites.

    For us, there is the obvious lesson of obeying God; things go better for us when we do. But there are also more subtle lessons about not judging others and the mercy of God. We should not have holier-than-thou attitudes like Jonah did toward the Ninevites. God loves everyone else just as He loves us. And because of that great love, there is no sin that is beyond God's mercy. He forgave the ruthless Assyrians. He will forgive any sin that is confessed with true sorrow and regret.

PRAYER
God, our merciful Father, we thank You for Your fathomless love for us and Your infinite mercy. You are a just God who demands punishment for sin, but You also grant mercy to anyone who asks for it. Help us to be like You. Make us a merciful people full of love for others, not just ourselves. Open a door today for us to show that love to someone in a tangible way.

Amen

#19 ISAIAH   (scroll, charcoal)

Isaiah 6:1-8; 9:56: 11:1-2

King Uzziah was a king of Judah, the southern kingdom. He reigned for 52 years and died, crippled with leprosy, in the year 742 B.C. That was the same year Isaiah received his call to become a prophet of God. He became the greatest of all the prophets and yet we know little of his private life. He lived in Jerusalem, the capital of Judah, married a prophetess, and had two sons. The book of Isaiah contains numerous prophecies about the Messiah.

The land of Israel was very tumultuous during the time of Isaiah. His career spanned the reign of three kings of Judah: Jotham, Ahaz and Hezekiah (#20 Hezekiah). Because of the people's idolatry, God punished them by sending foreign invaders.

The northern kingdom was conquered by the Assyrians in 722 B.C. The Assyrians were especially ruthless and effective, and their warfare tactics changed the way armies fought forever after. They were the first to have archers on horseback; they would charge with their chariots massed closely together; they would siege a city and keep it under constant arrow fire while weakening the walls by tunneling under them or building an earthen ramp to the top of the wall. They were also known to burn entire cities with everyone inside, impale people on stakes, and amputate limbs and heads.

In Israel, many people were killed, many others were deported to foreign countries, while people from other countries were imported to live in the land of Israel and intermarry with the local people. The Samaritans descended from this intermarriage and the pure-bred Jews despised them.

Isaiah warned the kings and the people of what was to come – that God would not allow their idolatry to go unpunished, but if they turned to Him for help He would save them from their enemies. When the kings ignored the advice of Isaiah, Assyria attacked and won. But when they followed Isaiah's advice, they were miraculously saved. Isaiah's prophecies warn the people of God's coming punishment and to repent of evil. He encourages them to trust in God, not political allies. He tells them people will be deported but a remnant of those faithful to God will survive and a Deliverer will come who will rule with justice – the Messiah. Hindsight is very good and we can see the fulfillment of those prophecies in Jesus.

The message for us is clear: Trust God. He is faithful. Even in times of political upheaval, God is in control. And He is just. He will not allow sinfulness to go unpunished, so we must make sure to repent of any sin in our lives.

PRAYER
Dear Jesus, You are our Messiah, our Wonder-Counselor, our God-Hero, our Prince of Peace. We praise You for Your providence and protection, and promises which You always keep. We thank You for Your justice and we ask that You would give us Your Spirit's gifts of wisdom, understanding, counsel, strength, and knowledge, so that we will always follow Your laws and always do what pleases You. And we know that if we do these things, You have promised to watch over us and protect us from evil.

Amen

#20 HEZEKIAH (king)

Isaiah 7:10-16

Ahaz was an evil king. He was 20 years old when he became king and he not only worshiped idols, he set up molten statues of them and offered his sons to be burned as sacrifices. He was king of Judah, the southern kingdom, and because of his idolatry, God raised up several enemies who attacked Judah; one of them being fellow Jews, the king and armies of Israel, the northern kingdom. The kings of Aram (present day Syria) and Israel wanted Ahaz to enter with them into an alliance against the dreadful Assyrians. But Ahaz refused, so Aram and Israel set out to attack Judah.

Isaiah advised Ahaz to trust God to deliver Judah from its attackers. He said, "Take care you remain tranquil and do not fear; let not your courage fail. Unless your faith is firm you shall not be firm! Ask for a sign from the Lord, your God." (Isaiah 7:4,9,10)

In a hypocritical way, Ahaz refused to ask for the sign. He preferred to trust in a political alliance instead of God, and he made that alliance with no one other than the Assyrians! It is very likely that it is really Ahaz's fault Israel was attacked and taken over by the Assyrians a few years later. (#19 Isaiah)

When Ahaz refused to ask for a sign, God told Isaiah to give him one anyway. It is the famous passage in today's scripture which we read every Advent, "The virgin shall be with child, and bear a son, and shall name him Immanuel." (vs.14) *Immanuel* means *with us is God.* (Remember in Hebrew *el* means *God.*) We, of course, recognize this as a prophecy about Jesus being born of Mary.

All Bible passages have a meaning for us today that we can see more clearly than the original writer because we have a bigger picture to look at, spanning many centuries. But they also have a meaning relevant to the time of their writing. At the time of Ahaz, this promise likely referred to the next king, Ahaz's son, Hezekiah. When Isaiah spoke this prophecy, Hezekiah's mother was not even married yet; she was a virgin.

Hezekiah turned out to be a good, Godly king who went through the land destroying all the altars his father had built for idol worship. Hezekiah was the only king to withstand a siege by the Assyrians. In the beginning of his reign, he had enlarged the aqueduct system into the city of Jerusalem, so when the Assyrians attacked and laid siege, the citizens inside the walls still had water. Isaiah advised Hezekiah to trust in God to deliver them. Hezekiah trusted and God delivered. Very mysteriously, one morning the Assyrians woke up in their tents and found 185,000 of their men had died during the night! They broke camp and went home to Nineveh. Isaiah prophesied that the Assyrian king would meet a bad end; he was murdered by his own sons.

Hezekiah is a type of the Messiah because he was a Godly king from the line of David who fought against evil and won. He encouraged his subjects to worship the one true God and to trust Him even in dire circumstances.

PRAYER

Lord Jesus, promised Son of the Virgin Mary, we adore You as our King. Give us courage and strong faith to withstand the attacks of evil. And help us to always trust in You as our Strong Deliverer.

Amen

#21 JEREMIAH (heart)

Jeremiah 23:5-8; 31:31-34

The land of Israel was a valuable piece of real estate and everybody wanted it. It was situated in the middle of a great trade route in ancient times: Egypt lay to the southwest, to the north and east were Assyria (present day Syria and northern Iraq) and Babylonia (present day Iraq and Kuwait), and the Mediterranean Sea bordered it on the west. Israel was constantly fighting off invaders from Egypt or empires from the north and east.

Jeremiah was called to be a prophet for the Lord in the year 628 B.C. There was a good king on the throne of Judah, Josiah, who had begun to reform the land and turn the people's hearts from their idol worship. But, sadly, he died while fighting the Egyptians. After his death, the people returned to their idolatrous ways, and Jeremiah warned them that God would punish them if they did not repent. Instead of repenting, they arrested Jeremiah and threw him into prison. Another time he was arrested and thrown into an empty well where he sank up to his armpits in mud. His words were not very popular, but they were true. He warned that the land would be conquered and their king would be carried off to a foreign land. And so it happened.

In 612 B.C., Assyria fell to Nebuchadnezzar, king of the Babylonian Empire. King Nebuchadnezzar also captured Jerusalem and carted away the king of Judah, leaving the king's uncle, Zedekiah, to rule. Zedekiah was the last king of Judah, the southern kingdom, whose kings had all followed the bloodline of King David. (The northern kingdom was no more, it had fallen to Assyria in 721 B.C.) In spite of Jeremiah's warnings, Zedekiah very foolishly revolted, causing Nebuchadnezzar to take swift vengeance by destroying Jerusalem in 587 B.C. and exiling all of the rich and the young and the beautiful to Babylon.

Jeremiah was left behind and continued to preach to the remnant of people who were still in the land. Just like Isaiah, his prophecies about the coming Messiah were meant to encourage them and give them hope in the midst of terrible circumstances. Today's passage from chapter 31 is sometimes called the *Gospel before the Gospel* because it refers to the New Covenant made by Jesus on the cross. The Old Covenant was made with Moses, who sealed the promise by sprinkling lamb's blood on a tablet of words. The New Covenant was sealed with the blood of Jesus, the Lamb of God.

According to tradition, not scripture, Jeremiah was taken as a captive to Egypt and then murdered. Also legend is the story that Jeremiah, who knew the Babylonians were coming and would destroy the temple, took the Ark of the Covenant and hid it in the mountains where it has never been found (unless you believe the Indiana Jones story). Or possibly, Nebuchadnezzar destroyed the Ark along with the temple. At any rate, it disappears from the historical scene here. The Ark contained Moses' original stone tablets of the Ten Commandments. We no longer have the original words of the Law in a physical form that we can touch. Now we have God's laws in our hearts. (Jeremiah 31:33)

PRAYER

Jesus, Lamb of God, You take away the sins of the world, have mercy on us. We thank You for the prophets you sent to prepare the way for Your coming. We thank You for Your justice that disciplines those who disobey You, but protects those who heed Your words. Help us to always keep Your law in our hearts and strive to please You.

     Amen

#22 DANIEL (lion)

Daniel 6:4-13, 20-24

Who doesn't love the story about Daniel in the lions' den? Another favorite story from this same setting is Shadrach, Meshach and Abednego in the fiery furnace, found in the second and third chapters of Daniel.

Yesterday we learned that the Babylonians, led by King Nebuchadnezzar, overtook the Assyrian empire and then proceeded to conquer all the surrounding lands, including Judah. Its capitol, Jerusalem, was destroyed in 587 B.C., and the young, the rich and the beautiful were deported to Babylon. This was called The Exile, and the very best among the exiled were hand-picked and trained to take positions in the Babylonian government. Daniel, along with Shadrach, Meshach and Abednego, were among those chosen.

Daniel was a visionary – he saw many visions and dreams about things to come and God blessed him with great wisdom to interpret dreams and solve disputes and other governmental problems. It did not take long for King Nebuchadnezzar to recognize Daniel as a valuable advisor. Daniel's Babylonian name was Belteshazzar.

In 539 B.C. Babylon was defeated and destroyed by Cyrus the Great, a Persian. Daniel had foretold this event in the story about the writing on the wall recorded in Daniel chapter 5. All the kings after Nebuchadnezzar, both Babylonian and Persian, sought Daniel's counsel and it often made the king's other advisors jealous. The lions' den story happened during the reign of Darius, who reigned after Cyrus.

Other well-known stories that happened during The Exile are those of Susanna (Daniel 13) and Esther, found in the book which bears her name.

The Persian Empire eventually fell to Alexander the Great in 331 B.C. And then, of course, we know that after that the Roman Empire became dominant. Daniel foresaw all of this changing landscape in his visions, dreams and interpretations of dreams.

Daniel also has prophecies about the Messiah. In Daniel 7:13-14 he says, "As the visions during the night continued, I saw One like the son of man coming, on the clouds of heaven; When he reached the Ancient One and was presented before him, He received dominion, glory, and kingship; nations and peoples of every language serve him. His dominion is an everlasting dominion that shall not be taken away, his kingship shall not be destroyed." Jesus often referred to Himself as the *Son of Man.* Salvation came through a man. In the prophecies, evil kingdoms opposed to God are always referred to as beasts.

PRAYER

God of all history, we know that You control all things. No king gains or loses power without Your decreeing it. In our own political arena, help us not to forget that. May we always be loyal as Daniel was, but also know that You are the only One who deserves our worship and total allegiance. No matter what chaos may be whirling around us, help us to have total trust in You.

Amen

#23 MALACHI (gold, silver)

Malachi 3:1-4

Malachi earns a place in our book because it is the very last book in the Old Testament; the last words we read before starting the genealogy of Jesus in the first chapter of Matthew. We know absolutely nothing about Malachi. Some scholars think it might be a *nom de plume,* a pseudonym for the author who did not want to use his real name. Still others think it is just a title taken from the third chapter. The Hebrew word *mal'aki* means *my messenger.*

When the Persians conquered Babylon, Kings Cyrus and Darius allowed the Jews to return to the land of Israel to live. In the first wave, 40,000 went, but many others stayed in Babylon. They had established good and prosperous lives in Babylon and didn't want to leave. Some Jewish families had lived in the area for nearly 200 years since the Assyrians first exiled them, and it was the only life they knew.

Those who returned to Jerusalem worked to rebuild the temple. It took them 20 years. Fifty years later, in 445 B.C., Nehemiah led a group of Jews back to rebuild the city walls. It was not easy, but they worked hard and finished a mere 52 days later, an amazing feat. God was truly with them. This time period is known as the Restoration and the story is told in the Old Testament books of Ezra and Nehemiah. Ezra was a dedicated priest who called the people to holiness.

During the 50 year period between the rebuilding of the temple and the rebuilding of the walls, the people in Jerusalem became complacent in their faith and lazy in the practice of their religion. The priests were not offering sacrifices in accord with the Law, the people were entering into illicit marriages, and they all had the nerve to blame God for not blessing them. In their defense, they had been in Babylon for many years, unable to offer sacrifices; they had forgotten how. They were not even able to read the Hebrew words on their scrolls anymore, so they were ignorant of the requirements of the Law. But they also made little effort to learn them.

Malachi was written as a sharp reproach to the priests and people, a warning that they were dishonoring God and so His judgment would come. Today's scripture passage tells the people that a messenger will come to prepare the way for the day of the Lord, the day of judgment. The messenger will call the people to repentance and true worship. When God appears, He will purify the nation in the furnace of His judgment. (If you are familiar with Handel's *Messiah*, you might recognize today's scripture reading as one of the solos. Astonishingly, Handel wrote the whole oratorio in less than a month!)

As we read this, it seems that Malachi himself, whatever his real name, is the messenger. Shortly after this was written, Ezra and Nehemiah arrived as messengers of reform. But we can look at a bigger picture and see that the true fulfillment of this passage was in John the Baptist, calling people to repent and be baptized. (#25 John)

Over and over throughout the Old Testament, we have seen the Israelites turn away from God and then God sends or threatens judgment and they repent and turn back to God. He always takes them back. His mercy is endless. We may find ourselves straying from God and His love. Repent. Plead for His mercy. We need pure and sinless hearts for the Christ child.

PRAYER

God of mercy, we come to You as imperfect beings, always feeling our hearts being pulled this way and that, often away from You. Please forgive us for straying and draw us back to You. Cleanse our hearts and make them pure so the Baby Jesus can dwell there when He comes.

#24 GABRIEL (angel)

Luke 1:5-38

We are finally reading out of the New Testament, a sure sign that Christmas is getting close. But today's person is not just a New Testament character. In fact, he is not even a person. Gabriel is a spirit – pure intelligence and will, but no body. His name means *might of God.* Only two other angels are named for us in scripture: Michael (*who is like God*), who seems to be the general of all the angelic armies, and Raphael (*God hath healed*), who took on a human form and helped Tobit and Tobias. (Some may wonder about Lucifer, but his name is only in Isaiah 14:12 and refers to the king of Babylon; the early church fathers used the name to refer to Satan.)

Notice that all of the angel names have *el* in them, the Hebrew word for God. The word *angel* also has *el* in it and means *messenger of God.* We refer to all the heavenly spiritual beings as angels, but technically, that is only the name of the lowest order of beings. Theologians think the Bible identifies higher orders as archangels, principalities, powers, virtues, dominations, thrones, cherubim and seraphim. We do not know how many there are, but the inference is that there are thousands and thousands, too many to count.

It seems to be Gabriel's job to come to earth and deliver specific messages from God. The first time he is named in the Bible is in Daniel 8:16, where he appears to Daniel and tells him the meaning of his vision. He is named again in Luke where he appears to Zechariah and then again to Mary, telling them they will have sons. Because some Old Testament birth announcements follow the same formula, we might assume that it was Gabriel who announced the births of Samson and Isaac.

The birth announcement formula is: 1. The angel appears. 2. The person is afraid and the angel tells him/her not to fear. 3. The birth is promised. 4. The child is named. 5. The future achievements of the child are told.

In today's scripture we read that John would be born rather miraculously of aged parents, and because of the angel and Zechariah's muteness and old Elizabeth conceiving a child, we sense that something spectacular is going to happen. Then the same angel appears to Mary and announces a virgin birth. The coming of the Messiah has finally been set in motion after Israel has waited for hundreds of years for the fulfillment of Isaiah's prophecies. Now we can start getting excited about His coming at Christmas!

PRAYER

Jesus, Lord of hosts, we thank you for the whole spirit world which exists simply to do Your bidding. Thank You for the awe and wonder the spirits cause in us as we contemplate their work. May we never take them for granted nor do things to work against them. We thank You for the spectacular events that surrounded Your coming to earth the first time and we wait with eagerness Your coming this Christmas.

Amen

#25 JOHN   (grasshopper, blue tissue paper = water)

Luke 3:1-18

John the Baptist is a very strange character. Yesterday we read about the unusual events surrounding his birth. Imagine you are a neighbor watching the events unfold. Zechariah returns from his temple duties unable to speak. Then his old wife becomes pregnant. A young cousin shows up for a long visit and we begin to realize she is also pregnant, but unmarried. At the circumcision, Zechariah miraculously gets his voice back. With all of these curious events, we wonder to what greatness John may aspire.

But then as an adult, we see him go out into the desert wilderness to live; he wears animal skins and eats grasshoppers. He is a madman! We would think people would avoid him, but instead people flock out to the desert to see and hear him and they feel the need to repent and be baptized.

We often think of water baptism as a purely Christian thing, but it is not. We believe that the waters of baptism actually wash away original sin. Washing away sin with water was not a new or novel idea for the early Christian Jews. In Deuteronomy 21 there is an interesting ceremony for the leaders of a city to perform if a murdered corpse is found and no one knows who is responsible (it could even be a wild animal). Because God requires justice, the city needs to avert God's judgment, so they wash away their guilt by cutting the throat of a heifer while holding it down in a running stream. The city leaders are to wash their hands in the water and say a prayer and their guilt is washed away with the heifer's blood down the stream.

Over and over again in the laws of Leviticus and Deuteronomy the priests and people are told to bathe in water either to wash away sin and ritual uncleanness or prepare themselves for a special event with God. Even today some Jews perform a ceremony on Rosh Hashanah (#1 Creation) called *tashlich,* which they perform next to a body of water in order to cast their sins from their souls into the water. They cite Nehemiah 8:1 where the people gathered by water for a ceremony after the walls of Jerusalem were rebuilt under the leadership of Nehemiah and Ezra (#23 Malachi).

In Leviticus 16 the high priest was required to bathe both before and after he went in to the Holy of Holies (#11 Tabernacle). Jesus, the Messiah, the true Holy of Holies was on earth and people needed to prepare themselves to be in His presence. The Old Testament prophets, especially Isaiah, foretold that someone would *prepare the way* for the Messiah. John seemed to know this was his job. He and Jesus were cousins, so we wonder when exactly he suspected who Jesus really was and when John realized his own role. In Luke 7 John sent messengers to ask Jesus to confirm that He was, indeed, the Messiah.

When Jesus was baptized of John, He had no sins to be washed away. But if He had not done that, we would be inclined to think we do not need baptism ourselves. We are to follow the example of Jesus in ALL things. Do we do that?

Do we, like the crowds who listened to John, have a need to repent so we have clean souls for the coming of the Savior?

PRAYER

Jesus, our Messiah and Redeemer, thank You for the rich history we have in the scriptures so we can see a bigger and clearer picture of our faith. Forgive us of any sin in our lives and help us to follow the rules set forth for us that help us to live lives pleasing to you. John, we ask for your intercession to help us feel conviction and regret over any sin we commit.

Amen

#26 MARY (Mary)

Luke 1:46-55

Today's scripture reading is often called the *Magnificat.* It is Mary's exclamation and praise to God upon meeting her cousin, Elizabeth, John's mother. It is possible that it is based upon a very old hymn that the Jews sang. In the Old Testament, Hannah, Samuel's mother, says, or perhaps sings, similar words when Samuel is born (1 Samuel 2:1-10).

A prominent theme in both canticles is that God lifts up the lowly. Over and over again throughout history, we have seen God use the lowliest and least likely person to accomplish His will. God loves a humble and willing heart.

Mary was chosen to be a vessel to hold God. She is an ark just like the Old Testament Ark of the Covenant which sat in the Holy of Holies and held the *shekinah*, the Glory of God. (#11 Tabernacle) Luke 1:35 says the Holy Spirit *overshadowed* Mary. The same word is used about the Transfiguration and several times in the Old Testament about the Ark of the Covenant, but is usually translated as a *cloud.* King David asked, "How can the ark of the Lord come to me?" (2 Samuel 6:9) and Elizabeth asked, "How does it happen to me that the mother of my Lord should come to me?" (Luke 1:43)

In 2 Samuel 6, during the reign of King David, the Ark of the Covenant spent three months in the house of Obededom the Gittite and his entire household and all of his flocks were blessed with fertility and prosperity. We do not know the exact location of Obededom's house, but it is in the same general area of Elizabeth's home and could be the exact same place. Mary, the Ark, spent three months with Elizabeth, during which time John was born. Elizabeth was old and the birth could have been very dangerous. But Mary's presence there, with God inside of her, ensured that John would be born safely, just like the family of Obededom.

Throughout these days of Advent, we have seen many examples of what we might call coincidences. But with God there is no such thing. He has everything planned down to the tiniest detail. All that is required is for us to say *yes* to Him, the same way Mary did.

PRAYER
Hail, Mary, full of grace, the Lord is with thee. Blessed art thou among women and blessed is the fruit of thy womb, Jesus. Holy Mary, Mother of God, pray for us sinners now, and at the hour of our death.
Amen

#27 JOSEPH (Joseph, dream catcher)

Matthew 1:18-25

Several weeks ago we took a look at the Old Testament Joseph, the son of Jacob who saved his family from a severe famine. (#8 Joseph) Today we consider the New Testament Joseph, foster-father of Jesus. Besides the same name, there are several other similarities between them.

The genealogy of Joseph is given in the first chapter of Matthew and we see that New Testament Joseph also had a father named Jacob.

Both Josephs were dreamers. Old Testament Joseph had dreams that told the future and he was able to interpret the dreams of others. New Testament Joseph had three dreams where angels appeared to him and told him what to do. (Matthew 1:20, 2:13, 2:19) Don't you sometimes wish an angel would come and tell you what to do?

Both Josephs went to Egypt to save their families from death. For Old Testament Joseph, a famine threatened the family with starvation. New Testament Joseph saved the child Jesus from the jealous King Herod who wanted to kill him by killing all of the baby boys in Bethlehem less than two years of age.

In Genesis 39, the wife of Joseph's master falsely accused Joseph of violating her. He was innocent, but sent to prison anyway. Mary was found to be pregnant before she married Joseph. It is very likely that most people blamed Joseph. He knew he was innocent, but if he declared that publicly, Mary would be punished. Old Testament penalties for this included everything from being cut off from the community to stoning to being burned to death. No wonder Joseph wanted to protect her. But when the angel told him to go ahead and take Mary for his wife, the angel was essentially telling him to take the blame from the public arena without protest. In a way, he was punished for a crime he did not commit just like Old Testament Joseph.

God does not always remove the misery from our lives. Sometimes we must bear it. But in the cases of both Josephs, we know the ends of the stories and know that because of them and their enduring God's will for them, wonderful things happened – entire worlds were saved. We don't know the end story of our lives yet. We need to trust in God that we too will have wonderful endings.

PRAYER
Our omnipotent and all-powerful God, we worship You and thank You for Your Providence. We commit ourselves to Your will and trust You to control our lives. As we welcome Your Son on Christmas Day, we stand in awe of the incredible events surrounding His coming. May we always see you as the awesome God that You are.
      Amen

#28 STAR (star)

Matthew 2:1-12

It is amazing that only the magi see the *Star of Bethlehem.* One would think that half the town of Bethlehem would be out following the bright star and finding the Baby Jesus in the manger. But signs are seen by those who look for them.

Most theologians think the magi came from Persia, present day Iran. As we have seen, many Jews spent many years in the Persian Empire, among them the Prophet Daniel, who was probably a magus himself. (#22 Daniel) Because the Jews were exported to other countries, their prophecies about a future king became known in those countries.

Although the Jews didn't practice astrology, the Persians did. There is a messianic prophecy in Numbers 24:17 that says a star will "advance from Jacob", accompanying the birth of the Messiah. So the stargazers in Persia were searching the night skies for a sign – a star.

Most astronomers have thought that the *Star of Bethlehem* was a comet or nova or supernova. But an astronomer named Michael Molnar* says it was the planet of Jupiter. There was an eclipse of Jupiter on April 17 in 6 B.C. It would have been visible in Persia but not in Jerusalem or Bethlehem. The star of Jupiter would have first appeared early in the morning and been hard to see in the morning light, but as days and weeks went by, it would have become brighter and higher. Because the earth rotates and orbits the sun, from earth it looks like the stars move backward (retrograde motion).

Molnar thinks the magi would have arrived in Jerusalem at Herod's court in October or November of 6 B.C.

No one knows for sure the exact day or month or year that Jesus was born. We do know that King Herod died in 4 B.C., so it was before that date. Molnar's date fits with this and the fact that Herod ordered the death of infants under two years of age. It is traditionally accepted that Jesus was born in our late December or early January. So he might have been born in 5 B.C. and returned from Egypt with his parents in 3 or 4 B.C. It was sometime in the 4th century A.D. that the Church chose December 25 to celebrate Jesus' birth.

The magi in Persia were looking for a great king to be born among the Hebrew people, and they studied the Hebrew Scriptures to find the prophecies about his coming. The Jewish scholars did the same. But while the Jews sat passively waiting for a great political leader to arrive on the scene; the magi were active, searching the skies for a star. And then they were very active in traveling a great distance to find the infant king. We have been looking for Him all through Advent. We will find Him. Hebrews 9:28 says that He will appear to those who look for Him.

**The Star of Bethlehem – The Legacy of the Magi* by Michael Molner; Rutgers University Press

PRAYER

Jesus, You are the Light of the World. You are the Infant King. You are the Promised Messiah. And You are God in the flesh. Help us to see You everywhere this Christmas; not just in the manger nativity scene, but in the joy of the season; in those around us, the needy and the not-so-needy; and, mostly, in our own hearts.

Amen

#29 JESUS (baby)

Luke 2:1-16

Merry Christmas! It's finally here – the day for which we have been waiting! The Messiah is finally born!

Messiah is a Hebrew word meaning *anointed one* and *Christ* is the Greek word with the same meaning. In the Old Testament, priests and kings were anointed when they began their vocations. Jesus is both a priest and a king. He is also a prophet and a judge.

Deuteronomy 17 and 18 set forth the rules and requirements for those who would be judges, kings, priests and prophets. Reading through these, we can see that many of the characters we have been looking at these past weeks failed miserably to meet the criteria. But Jesus fulfills them all.

In Exodus 30:23-25 we find the recipe for the anointing oil used on the priests and kings in Israel. The main ingredient is myrrh. And in verses 34-35 we have the recipe for incense which uses pure frankincense. We know that the magi brought these as gifts along with gold. It does seem quite likely that they anointed the Baby Jesus the myrrh oil and burnt incense for Him.

Jesus said He came to fulfill the law (Matthew 5:17) and He did so in every way. He was perfect. But He came to the earth as a baby in poverty and humility, so that no one could say He was only meant for the rich or powerful or famous or mature. He is all things for all people. Who can resist a cuddly baby? Who doesn't want to pick Him up and warm him from the chilly air and give him a better bed than a manger? Who cannot wonder at the incredible visitors – humble and despised shepherds and wealthy, respected wisemen from faraway lands? And what about his parents? There is incredible awe accompanying any birth along with the thoughts of what an overwhelming job parenting will be. Mary & Joseph must have been positively overcome!

It has been a long wait for us, but not as long as the Jewish people waited! We have heard that old saying *good things come to those who wait.* We are expecting good things today – very, very good things. God Himself is with us!

PRAYER

Dear Baby Jesus, thank You so much for coming to earth and taking on human form so You can be like us. Thank You for coming in humility, with all of Your splendor as king and priest and prophet hidden. Thank You for the written Word, so we can see for ourselves the story that leads to You. And thank You for today, Your birthday, when we can celebrate all of the good things that You have given us.

                    Amen